Gross Greg

Story by
ALVIN IRBY

Pictures by
KELVIN NTUKULA

Author's Note

Teaching kindergarten and first grade, my students and I laughed a lot. Learning was fun and funny. Gross Greg celebrates the joy of childhood in its purest and grossest form. Gross Greg invites children and adults to laugh about and reflect on what it means to be a child.

Copyright © 2019 by Alvin Irby
All right reserved. No part of this publication, except for brief review, may be reproduced, distributed, or transmitted in any form, or stored in a database or retrieval system, without prior written permission from the publisher.

Published by Alvin Irby LLC
P.O. Box 1752, New York, NY 10035
Visit website at www.grossgreg.com

Illustrations by Kelvin Ntukula
Book design by Shawn Hazen

Printed in China
First Printing, May 2019

Irby, Alvin.
Gross Greg/ by Alvin Irby ; Illustrated by Kelvin Ntukula.

ISBN 978-0-9977818-0-9 (hardcover)
ISBN 978-0-9977818-2-3 (softcover)
ISBN 978-0-9977818-1-6 (Ebook)

New York : Alvin Irby LLC, 2019. | Series: Gross Greg.
Summary: A humorous rhyming story about a boy who loves eating his boogers.
Humorous Stories. | African Americans – Juvenile Fiction.
JUV019000 JUVENILE FICTION / Humorous Stories

PZ7.1
DDC [E] – dc23

To my mom, Jacqueline Irby, for inspiring me to teach and to my nephew, Torrance, for inspiring me to write this book
– A. I.

To my father, Peter Ntukula
– K. N.

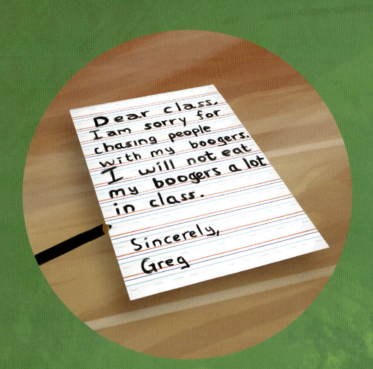

Bam! Bam! Bam!

Greg hears three loud knocks on his bedroom door.

Now Greg knows he can't sleep anymore.

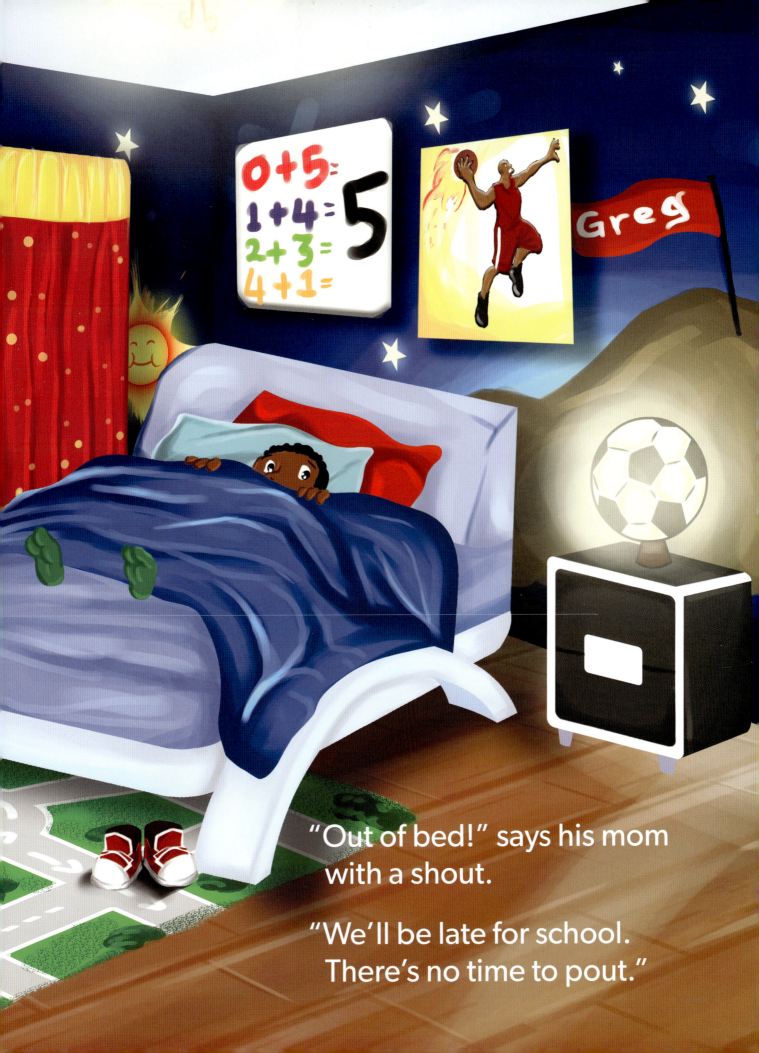

"Ahhhhhhhh."

With a loud yawn, he's up on his feet.

Greg's eyes are still sleepy, but he wants something to eat.

Look!

Outside his window, a long line can be seen.

Adults wait at the coffee cart for many sweet things.

Yummy cinnamon rolls, donuts, and muffins are there.

But what Greg wants for breakfast gives most kids a scare.

He doesn't want mustard covered pancakes or pickle-flavored cereal. That would be weird.

Greg craves chewy yellow and green nuggets that are usually feared.

You call them boogers.

Greg calls them delicious little sugars.

Do you eat your boogers? Greg thinks you should.

At least one a day, that would be good.

Boogers during the summer satisfy his appetite just fine.

But if you ask Greg for one, he'll respond, "No! They're all mine!"

"They taste just like chicken," Greg loves to say.

"Ewwwwwww," screams his little sister as she runs away.

"Greg's being gross!" she complains to Dad.

"If you're eating your boogers again, I'm going to get mad."

Oh yeah!

Gross Greg is the name he loves to hear.

To him, it sounds like a cool basketball cheer.

"Gross - Greg! Gross - Greg!

This name is not an insult. It's a source of pride, even when his classmates run and hide.

"Greg!"

"Stop eating your boogers" says his teacher in disgust.

"Go to the sink, wash your hands, and stop making a fuss."

Greg loves math because he likes to count.

When his teacher isn't looking, he collects boogers until he reaches the perfect amount.

Greg 4/8/16

Greg's Math Number Story:

4 + 2

Greg ate four boogers then he ate two more. How many boogers did Greg eat all together?

Oh no!

"One booger. Two boogers. Three boogers. Four."

Greg would keep counting, but he has no more.

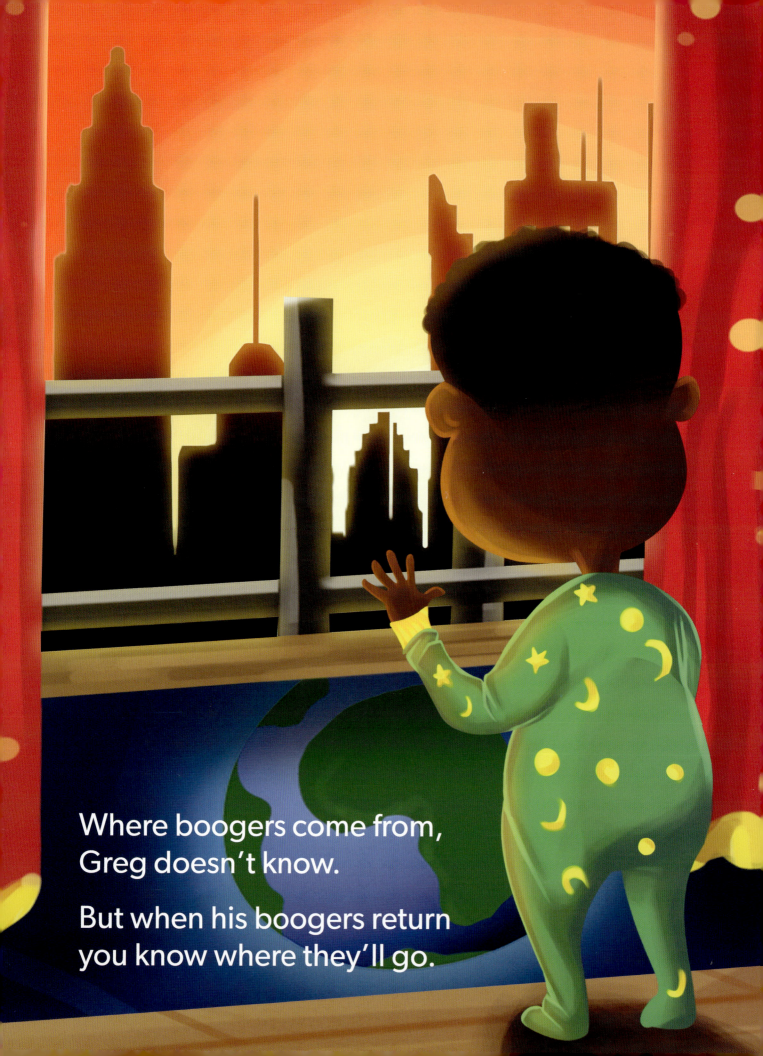

Where boogers come from, Greg doesn't know.

But when his boogers return you know where they'll go.